Breathing Just A Little…

Breathing Just A Little

Bismillah,

from all of my softness,
to all of yours.

Contents

One: Breathing just a little	**page 8**
To be easy	page 9
Gemini	page 10
Blossom	page 11
Something makes me careful	page 12
The grass is always greener	page 13
Solemn	page 14
Body of regret	page 15
Barely here	page 16
Something, somewhere is calling	page 17
Present	page 18
Purpose	page 19
Muffle	page 20
Out of reach	page 21
Worthy	page 22
Absent	page 23
Normal	page 24
The lost days	page 25
Relative	page 26
Whose standard	page 27
Haunted	page 28
Here	page 29
Two: Holes in my chest	**page 30**
Holes in my chest	page 31
We are not so brave	page 32
The kind of girl	page 33
In my darkest hours	page 34
Stillness	page 35
This is how you keep us	page 37
The next time you fall in love	page 38

Suspended	page 39
The loving in us	page 40
A hundred lifetimes	page 41
Premonition	page 42
He said	page 43
Third eye	page 44
Grey heart	page 45

Three: Something falls away — **page 46**

Do you think of me?	Page 47
Something fell inside	page 48
People do not stay	page 49
When love is lost, surrender	page 50
Do not stay	page 51
The ones who haunt our days	page 52
We forget who we were	page 53
When trust is broken	page 54
Waitful	page 55
Wishing well	page 56
Away from the crowd	page 57
Someone I don't have to hide from	page 58
It has always been this way	page 59
Situation-ships	page 60
Self love as healing	page 61
Falling in love with my friends	page 62
What is it about staying	page 63
How to hold things	page 64
The tightness in our lungs	page 65

Four: The loneliness — **page 66**

I am always intruding	page 67
Things I want to tell you	page 68
Quality over quantity	page 69
Hiding my softness	page 70

Lonely is heavy	page 71
Immortal	page 72
The silence	page 73
Saving time	page 74
Old friend	page 75
To stretch my being	page 76
Tired	page 77
Conundrum	page 78
Lessons in quietude	page 79
How quiet I've become	page 80
Eclipse	page 81
Keep on; strong	page 82
Five: Belonging	**page 83**
Home	page 84
Split down the middle	page 85
Diluted	page 86
Colonized	page 87
In finding God	page 88
Ode to Amy Winehouse	page 89
Seeing red	page 91
Target	page 92
What I know of war	page 93
Nuura	page 94
My first love	page 96
Revere me	page 97
Enigma	page 98
Chains around my ankles	page 99
Alight	page 100
English as a second language	page 101
Lit	page 102
Soul break	page 103
Do not forget me too quickly	page 104

In memory of   page 105
Detachment   page 106

Six: The light   **page 107**
Resurrection   page 108
The quite   page 109
Blossom   page 110
Loneliness is a human condition   page 111
You will never be more alive   page 113
Dance   page 115
Finding love within   page 116
The hardest lesson   page 117
Take a little time for you   page 118
Be still   page 119
Al this world awaiting   page 120
Lovers in love   page 122
Tender mouth; fierce heart   page 123
A sign from God   page 124
Stillness as healing   page 125
The voices in your head   page 126

Seven: Softness   **page 128**
We are soft   page 129
All of my softness   page 130
Come as you are   page 131
How you look to me   page 132
Drown   page 133
Up in flames   page 134
Writing as letting go   page 135
Speak   page 136
Grounded   page 137
Love in truth   page 138
Gone   page 139
Let the current guide you   page 140

My woman is power	page 141
In the quiet hours	page 142
Guarding my heart	page 143
The strongest of men	page 144
With time we forget	page 145
In silence is truth	page 146

Breathing just a little

I am not easy. I want to be easier. First meeting laughter and conversation.
I want to be heartfelt hugs with strangers and deliberate handshakes.
I want to be soft and sultry, all 'babe' and 'darling' and 'what's cooking good looking?'

I want to be 'let's do dinner this evening', last minute plans and ease.
But I am not easy.

I am slow and delicate. Words on a text message checked three times before sending.
I am anxious, replaying conversations. Over and over.
And I am faltering.
All: 'hey…um… are you busy? I..err… was gonna' go and do something. But you don't have to if you don't want to…' apologetic, pathetic.

I am all heaviness and weight. All dragging my being through life.
I want to be easy. To float through life. light and air. Love and grace.
I want to be easy.

- To be easy

Breathing Just A Little

There are days I am fully there;
bubbling and bursting with life,
where conversation feels like
the most natural thing
and my instinct first
is to hug and kiss,
and dance with anyone
who is near and dear,
I am alive and here.
And then there are days like today,
where I begin to drift away
and the words in my head need
all the energy in my body to speak,
I feel weak and distant;
all I want is to retreat to a space,
that is quiet and warm,
where I am alone
and breathing is easy.
It seems as though I am
two opposing beings
vying to live in a single body.
even I,
do not know
which version will show,
each day.

- Gemini

Sometimes,
we let our bodies
become breeding grounds
for sadness.

We do not see
all the beauty
trying to grow within us-
around us.

- **Blossom**

Some nights sleep does not come and I am left
suspended between slumber and wake; heart full of
more than mind is able to put into words.
Some days I miss everything. Things I have known
and things I have not. Friendship. Evening walks.
Romance. Phone calls into the AM.
Sometimes I want to be outside at these hours. 1am,
or 2 or 3. On a rooftop, overlooking a busy city.
Lights and people in the distance.
Somehow I think that is where I belong. On the edge.
Close enough to witness life, but not near enough to
live it. Safe. Easy. comfortable.
Something inside makes me careful.
The same thing that causes my lonely.

- **Something makes me careful**

I am always convinced
that others are happier
than I am.
That perhaps they
know something more
about life and living
than I do.
Maybe -
there is a lesson
I have missed.
Perhaps -
there is a secret
I am yet to learn.

- **The grass is always greener**

Some days,
I do not want to smile.
Some days I am solemn,
for no reason at all.
And all I want is
to sit at the furthest corner
of a busy room and watch.
That is all.
Just watch.
Sometimes this is enough.

- Solemn

I hold regret in my heart
for the moments I could've made
into something bigger, deeper,
more beautiful,
my heart pumps longing into my body.

I carry apologies in my mouth;
my tongue is swollen with things
I should've said to the people I've loved;
who are now all too far in either body or heart to reach.

And my mind -
the space behind my eyes
is a gallery of lost chances,
my dreams have all become exhibitions
of things I've failed to achieve.

I feel the years weighing down on my body;
I look in mirrors and find only ghosts.

What kind of peace can there be,
for a soul like mine?

- Body of regret

Breathing Just A Little

Sometimes I am saddened
by how gently I live,
how thin,
how subtle;
how barely I exist.

And I am afraid.

I am terrified that perhaps
I am not capable
of living any other way.

- **Barely here**

I wander on the same path
and keep on coming back
to the same place.

I have been here my whole life.
I have been this person all along.
And I cannot find a way forward.

Maybe this is about God.
Maybe this about love or dreams.

Most days I feel as though there is somewhere I am
meant to be going. Something I am meant to do.
And I cannot find my way to it.

And yet somehow, I feel like I know it;
deep down, I feel like I have always known it.

Maybe, this is about everything, after all.

- **Something, somewhere is calling**

My spirit wanders -
I exist somewhere
between coming
and going,

almost -
I am almost here.

- **Present**

Some days
it is the things
I hold beautiful,
necessary and vital that crush me;
that pull me into despair
and cut me down in half.

My culture, my faith, my family.

Some days, everything
is chains around
my ankles, my throat, my lungs.

I am static;
I am small,
I am wrong.

These days,
I cannot remember
what anything means.

- **Purpose**

I am always plagued
by self doubt.

There is a choir in my head,
their voices too loud
to be ignored.

"Perhaps if I was other than I am,
perhaps if I did not look like I do,
perhaps if I was in some other body,
in some other place and time."

How do I muffle
this mind of mine?

- **Muffle**

Do not fall for me
because I am not easy.

I am not soft delicate warmth -
there is nothing easy about my composition.

I am part fleeting hurricane and consuming ocean.

I am not slow gentle heat,
but part searing mouth and jagged heart.

Do not fall for me,
I am not easy to love.

I am best kept
just out of reach.

- **Out of reach**

I am quick to love,
but slow in allowing myself
to be loved.

Love pours out from me
like waterfalls
and bursting river banks,
but comes towards me;
in slow droplets and thin trickles.

My dam's too sturdy.
something in the mind I think,
something tells me I am not worthy.

- **Worthy**

Sometimes I feel
as if I am not here,
fully.

I am always
away with myself,
elsewhere.

- **Absent**

Tonight I miss myself,
all of the parts
I have left on a shelf
and forgotten about.

Tonight, I am regretful
of conforming;
for all of this normal
I have squeezed
my heart inside,
folded my soul into.

Tonight, I am all the things
I was told that I should be;
but none of those
I have always wanted to.

- **Normal**

I do not know
what I have done today,
at all.
The hours have passed,
one after the other
and there has not been a single thing,
I could tell you that I have done.

I do not know
how it is
this happens.

How whole days can disappear before me;
curling up and crumpled away
somewhere in the distance.

And I will never have these days again.

- **The lost days**

I'd like to be the kind of beautiful that is terrifying,
aching, possessing.
The kind of exotic that enamors, enraptures and
mesmerizes.
I'd like to be the kind of woman men have eyes for,
to be the look of longing on a face,
the unconscious licking of lips,
the hairs standing on the back of necks,
the words they'd struggle to find.

I'd like to be that kind of beautiful,
even for a day;
I'd like to know how it feels.
But I am the kind of beautiful that is relative- earth
shattering to some,
non-existent to others.

The kind of beautiful that comes and goes,
the kind that fills you up to bursting some days,
then steals the air right out from your lungs.
I am the kind of beautiful,
that even I struggle some days to find.

- **Relative**

What does it mean, beauty?

Am I not enough
to fit your standards,
or are your standards
too small
to encompass all I am?

- **Whose standard**

Some thoughts settle inside you,
don't they?
Become part of who you are.

What can I do with these thoughts then?
that come around so often
it's as if they never leave.

How do I erase the very things
I am always creating?

- **Haunted**

Soft;
tonight I am a tender sort of alive.
and the night carries
a loving kind of silence,
tonight;
my heart pulses with it all
and it is enough that I am here.
that we are here.
tonight;
it is everything.

- **Here**

Breathing Just A Little

Holes in my chest

I have a habit of falling in love
with souls who have yet to be at peace
with their bodies, their minds,
their weaknesses.

I try to build them, to find the parts of them that are missing, in me.
I end up with holes in my chest.

- **Holes in my chest**

Love is not only that which is spoken.
And that which is spoken is not always love.

There are many people I pray for silently,
admire secretly;
there are people I have loved with a burning
intensity,
but chosen to keep hidden in the confines of my
chest,
a slow burning heat.

Because we are not so brave some of us.
But lovers nonetheless.
And loving just as hard.

- **We are not so brave**

I am the kind of girl
who thinks
about love
and writes
about love
but avoids
all the boys
she could
fall in love
with,
then
wonders
why
she is
always
alone.

- **The kind of girl**

Breathing Just A Little

If love exists,
let it find me in the quiet hours,
the dead of night.
Let it come to me
in the alleyways,
the empty, frightening spaces.
Let it shield me from rain,
sheath me from storms;
And protect me from the shadows.

If love exists-
let it not burn
only on the summer days.
I have known romance
to quickly spark amidst the haze
and burn out flat in darkness.
If love exists,
let it find me beautiful
in my darkest hours.

- **In my darkest hours**

Degenaan/Xasilooni

in Somali, this means:

'calmness', 'stillness', 'peaceful'.

-

I am drawn to men with calm faces,
silent bodies and still eyes.
Men with peaceful aura's that suggest
they must know God better than most-
must practice patience,
and prayer longer than most.

Men who do not anger easily,
but are able to contain inside themselves raging
storms-
who only whisper weightless angst
into the bosom of their lover at night.

I have always known,
that one of these days-
I will fall for the calming voice and companionable
silence
of a man who collects words
in order to thatch together meaningful speech
and beautiful thoughts.

And he will be the father of my children,
and they will resemble him more than me,
none of my swinging moods and jagged tongue
but all of his gentle strength.

- **Stillness**

I loved him because he was kind
and gentle-
soft even in all his rugged manliness.
a man must lay his
butch at the door
of a woman's heart-
softly treading,
gently loving,
quietly learning.
this is how you keep us.

- **This is how you keep us**

The next time you fall in love,
remember that flowers are living,
but still we pick them.

We tear them out from the Earth as if everything beautiful,
exists only to be admired, touched, smelt.

But beautiful things have feelings too;
an ache for home and roots, a place to belong and bloom.

How many flowers have seen death in your hand?
How many plants wilted because you only half loved them?
Housed in a jar, on a windowsill?

Do not forget this lesson,
do not imagine you can love a beautiful thing temporarily.

- **The next time you fall in love**

I don't know where the words have gone. Where all
the time and energy
and spirit, have gone.

There are parts of me everywhere;
left with everyone I have been with.
I am trying to find something in me, anything still
left of myself,
to hold onto.

- **Suspended**

I am searching for a place
that is soft;
a city that is warm and tender.

I am looking for people
who are gentle;
eyes full of compassion.

I am dreaming of a world,
where protecting each other;
is as important as protecting our forests.

I am looking for humanity.
I am looking for softness.
I am looking for the loving in us.

- **The loving in us**

We have lived
a hundred different lifetimes
- you and I -
together in my head;
every single one
a softer, more loving version
than the reality
in which we exist.

- **A hundred lifetimes**

n

You will be hurt
more often
than you will be loved,
and I am sorry that this is true.

- **Premonition**

He said,
he believed in love,
more than he believed
that the sky was blue.

Said the feelings in his heart,
were truer than the world
and all of its hues,

I said darling,
do you know how long,
I've been waiting for you?

- **He said**

I see too much.
I am always noticing everything,
the minor details,
the unspoken feeling,
the subtle signal of the nervous,
the truth that lurks beneath the surface.

My third eye is sharp; intuitive,
too precise to look at mortals with.

I am always pretending not to have seen
the things I notice naturally.

- **Third eye**

The grey skies are
a reflection of
my weathered heart.

- **Grey heart**

Breathing Just A Little

Something falls away

I imagine you must think of me at these times,
at these hours-
you must lay in bed,
one arm beneath your head-
and wonder 'bout all the things I must be doing.
All the people I must have met,
all the men I could be falling in love with,
all the mouths I might have kissed after you.

I imagine you must be doing this,
tossing and turning.
Are you doing this?

- **Do you think of me?**

When you become incredibly close
with someone, anyone
and suddenly they pull away....

It feels like something -
fell inside you,
doesn't it?

Like something fell away?

- **Something fell inside**

My dear
you must
stop
fixating
on
people.
fixate on objects.
books.
films.
never people.
people do not stay.

- **People do not stay**

Do not fight for someone that doesn't want to be yours.
Never hold on to someone that wants to leave.
Never ask them to stay.
Do not ask if they are coming back
Let them go.
Make it easy.
Tell them not to worry,
That you'll be okay and you were just not meant to be.
That you understand.
Even if you are a storm brewing,
clench your teeth to keep from shouting.
Curb your anger.
The questions.
Watch them walk away.
Do not let them see you cry.

- **When love is lost, surrender**

You will know when the time to leave comes,
you will be able to recognize the signs;
look for the nights that laughter
becomes swallowed by sighs,
the days when there is more tired
in your eyes; than life -

make note of the heavy in your bones,
the reluctance in your voice.
Keep mental counts of all the regret,
all the chances you have somehow let -
pass you by.

And when the ache in your heart,
threatens to tear your chest apart -
do not stay a moment longer.

When the time to leave comes,
you must go -
do not ignore the signs,
do not stay a moment longer.

- **Do not stay**

It is the ones who live in our minds that haunt us
the most -
the ones we walk away from,
all broken and lost without.

The ones we tell the world,
we have forgotten all about,
gotten over -
the ones we fix our lips
into forced smiles
to speak about in public.

Our hidden ghosts,
the ones we carry around inside us,
that we are all still trying to forget.

- **The ones who haunt our days**

We hold onto people
because we are afraid to let them go.
Not because we want them or need them. But
because we don't know how to be without them.
We forget who we were,
before we became the person we are with them.
Often, we don't even remember
that version of ourselves
and we have no idea
how to go back to being just us,
alone.

- **We forget who we were**

Lately-
I do not feel
as though
my name is safe
in the mouths
I once
trusted
with it.
and I do not know
how to ask for it back.

- **When trust is broken**

I find that most people do not care
for friendship
or the intensity of a complete connection.

Most want to know as many people as possible,
to be seen in as many places
with as many new acquaintances-
all friendly face but little heart.

But I want to know a few people intimately,
one or two-
to know them completely, vitally,
all open heart surgery and warm embraces.

And this is why I do not have many friends
and yet more smiling faces than I can put names to.

this is why I am always seeking sincerity-
I am always *waitful*, watchful,
careful who I share myself with.

- **Waitful** *[a feeling of always waiting]*

It seems
that I am a wishing well
for people to drop their worries into.

I collect pain and hardship,
pennies filling my chest.

But even a wishing well needs maintenance;

Even I need a friend.

- **Wishing well**

Sit with me,
just us alone,
Somewhere away from the crowd -

There is no honesty there,
All keeping face and loud and proud.

Sit with me,
just us alone,
Somewhere away from the crowd.

- **Away from the crowd**

I mean, I just want to lay in some grass land with someone, who'll tell me stories and let me lay my head on their lap or stomach.

I mean, I just want to know about somebody; everything. Right down to their core.

I mean, I'm tired of all this half knowing people; and half guessing who they are. Always being careful what I say.

I mean, I just want to know somebody that way. Properly. To be able to see them with clarity; even when they try to hide from me.

I guess, I think that's what love is and friendship, family; not feeling like you have to hide, and knowing you couldn't hide from that person even if you wanted to.

I mean, I guess that's what I want. Someone I don't have to hide from.

- **Someone I don't have to hide from**

I see the world over there, in the distance.
I see the people.
I hear the laughter and life being lived.

Some days I ache to be among them; in the midst of all the noise.

And others, I want to be as far as possible from it.

It has always been this way.
And it will always,
I think,
remain the same.

- **It has always been this way**

Most people
want so badly
to belong,
that they will choose
situation-ships
over sincere
friendship.

And I am the fool,
who is always
mistaking
the two;
loading all my heart
on ships that
never intended
to stay.

- **Situation-ships**

Truth is, I crave people.
I crave the memories,
the moments, the feelings.

My entire body almost wills itself back to people and places. Some nights, I have to tell it to be still.
To hold still a moment.

Have you ever had to do that? Talk your body and heart out of somebody? Soft like a whisper, warm winter shower, reminding it;

"they are not good for us baby.
they don't love us like we love them.
they don't need us the same.
we can't go back there again."

- **Self love as healing**

I am a little bit ridiculous and far too intense.

I seek friends the way most do lovers,
in heaving rooms, across packed dinner tables-
looking for faces that are kind, eyes that are honest
bodies that have no arrogance.

I ask too many questions, stare too hard.
I smile too much and I am always touching
on backs and arms, leaning my head on shoulders,
sharing just a little too much and eliciting even
more.

I am a little bit ridiculous and far too intense, the
way I fall into other souls, find homes for each in my
heart. The way I am always falling in love with all of
my friends.

But I do not understand, why anyone would keep
friends they weren't in love with?

- **Falling in love with my friends**

What is it about staying,
that is so hard for some?
What is it that makes them run,
tail between their legs
and promises in their mouth?

What is it about staying,
That is so frightening?
When there is love,
And softness -

What is it that makes
people leave in search of more?

- **What is it about staying**

I don't know how to hold things yet:

1 - Eye contact; with anyone who is seeking and searching, looking for something in me, to hold onto themselves. I don't know how to hold a gaze, when others are looking in me for the same things I am in need of myself.

2 - Hands, when they are shaking. When they are warm and pulsing; afraid. I don't know how to hold mine steady and brave against someone else's, how to caress and calm and soothe; when my hands are shaking with them.

3- A conversation, when it is new. When it is less breaking ice, more tiptoeing over sleet and silence and distance; the threat of falling [into silence] looming.

4- People, when they don't know how to stay.
I don't know how to hold things yet.
I don't know how to keep things together.

- **How to hold things**

I am stuck in a conversation
with someone I was once very close to
and we are stepping over eggshells,
choosing our words carefully.

There is a pool filling up around us;
all of the words we want to say but do not,
want to ask but do not.

We are both pretending
we do not notice
the tightness
in our lungs.

- **The tightness in our lungs**

Breathing Just A Little

The loneliness

I can never quite
get rid of the feeling;
that I am always intruding
into other people's lives.
I am always waiting
for permission
and sometimes;
I end up waiting
far too long.

- **I am always intruding**

1.

I am always loneliest when the night is at its darkest. And even more so when the first light breaks.

2.

There are things I want to tell someone, that I'm unable to share with anyone else. Little things that hardly matter at all, like how I woke up this morning desperate to pee; how I walked in the garden, bare feet and all the clouds floating away, made me want to leave, again.

3.

I wanted to pick flowers for all of my friends, before I mowed the garden. There were pink and yellow and white flowers too. But I wasn't sure how long, it would be, how many days will pass, before I saw anyone else.

4.

I wonder if everyone feels as lonely as I do.
I cannot imagine they could.

5.

There is a boy, who makes me think that marriage could work out well. And yet, there is no-one there for me to tell these things to.

- **Things I want to tell you**

I am finding
that the more people
I meet –

the less friends
it feels,
I have.

- **Quantity over quality**

I am lonely,
because I always feel
the need to hide my softness;
my anxious,
my timid and sad.

I wrap layers of politeness
and distance around
all of my tender.
I bruise easy
but heal in difficulty.

I do not know many
who will tread softly.
Who will know how to handle me.

- **Hiding my softness**

Lonely is a heavy thing.

I cannot think
of a better way to describe it.

It is heavy.

And always,
I feel its weight on my body.

- Lonely is heavy

I think about you in pieces, segments, snapshots. Your eyes. mouth. lips. collar bones. neck and back.

I think of you some days too much, far more than I should. It surprises me how much of you I remember-
(the sound of your voice, the curve of your eye lashes) and it terrifies me how much of you I've forgotten.

You have become a consuming silence. The space between sentences, the emptiness. The distant expression that falls over my face each time I remember you, quietly. in secret.
-
I am still learning how to immortalize people in memory. But you are fading fast and I am afraid that soon, there will nothing left of you to hold on to.

- Immortal

Sometimes
the silence
lulls me,

and sometimes,
it rocks me
to my core.

- The silence

I think that time,
is the greatest thing
we can give to anyone," she said.

"our time and our energy,
and we should give it wholly,
completely to the ones
we are giving it to."

"I don't know what could be worse;
what could be more difficult,
than having saved up all of your time,
for someone who does not save
any of theirs for you."

"What do I do with all of this time?
and all of this energy?
where do I put it now?

- Saving time

Sadness-
it comes sometimes doesn't it?

Quietly,
like an old friend."

- Old friend

Breathing Just A Little

The quiet is good, the alone necessary.
Every minute, of every day
I negotiate with others;
where I fit, the space I fill,
how much I speak, the words I use,
how much I show of who I really am.

I am always negotiating.

And so, it is a blessing the quiet,
necessary; the alone.
To switch off;
To stretch my being
in every direction,
without want of permission.

- **To stretch my being**

Some days I feel
there is nothing
inside me;
I am hollow to my bones,
empty.

And some days I feel
there is everything;
I am swollen with it all,
bursting.

I do not know yet
which is worse;
to feel too much
or not at all.

But it is tiring.
I know only this;
that it is tiring.

- **Tired**

Breathing Just A Little

> My alone
> is both my best friend
> and worst enemy.
>
> **- Conundrum**

I am learning
the art of quietude;
the mathematics
of silence as a weapon;
the science
of quietness as defense.

I am perfecting
the philosophy of stillness,

I am mastering
the geography of my heart;
I am unraveling
a lifetimes history of unbalance.

- **Lessons in quietude**

Some time passes
and I realize
how quiet
it has been.

Everything;
inside.
How quiet
I have become.
How softly -
Setting sun,
the noise
has gone.

- **How quiet I've become**

My soul is waiting,
patient as the moon -
to align with yours."

- **Eclipse**

I do not regret a thing.

I will cherish every bit of life
I have lived
and just as I have lived it.

What goodness is there
in looking back,
what change can come
from doing that?

- **Keep on; strong**

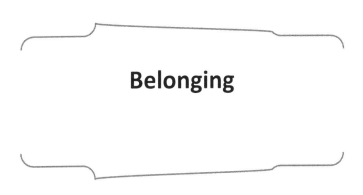

Belonging

I have heard the word "home" spoken around
me more often than any other word in my lifetime;
heard it spoken thick with longing,
my mother's tongue; slick with the accent of her
ancestors, her dialect still potent, fragrant; lingering.

We are the sons and daughters of lands that will
always be called "home." The children whose skins
lay testament to a place we may never have known;
who in broken attempts at our mother tongues,
still claim the lands that expelled us.

We are the in-betweeners - lost in a space between
being and belonging,
the lingering roots of a tree pulled from its soil. We
are sired to 'homes' we have never been to. Pained by
memories we can never lay claim to; more loyal to
the 'homes' we have left than the lands we have
moved to.

We are here, but we are not.
We are here, but we are not.

- **Home**

My dilemma in life
has always been this;
I am split down the middle.
I am part shy,
obedient woman of faith
with dreams of heaven and honour

and part flighty anarchist;
an unquenchable thirst for all things desirable.
I am only ever one or the other.
I have yet to find a balance.

- Split down the middle

Sometimes,
there is more English in me
than I can stand;

some days I cannot find
all of my mother tongue
and I cringe,

how polluted my mouth
has become,
how diluted my identity.

[we betray our mother tongues,
for the languages
of nations
that will never
fully accept us.

We let the strangeness
infest our mouths
until we forget
how to accommodate
our original tongues]

- Diluted

There are walls everywhere,
between us all
invisible; but always there.

- **Colonized**

Some people,
in finding God -
lose their softness.
Their gentle and loving.

What road did you take
to get to Him?

What war did you encounter
that left you cold and hard?

What made you lose
all the laughter,
all the sweetness and light?

- **In finding God**

Dear Amy,

Did you ever imagine someone like me
would find a home
in your mournful melodies
and sombre voice?

That you could fill voids
in the hearts of muslin girls
trying desperately to be women?

Did you know that-
we used to sneak into our living room at night
and listen to you;
crouched by the corner of our sofa,
knees pulled up to our chests,
our hijjabs wrapped high above our heads
so we could pretend we had hair like you?

Amy,
do you know how much you meant to us?
We never knew pain until you,
never knew addiction until we saw you wither away;
imagined you;
heart all over the kitchen floor.

You taught us more about love than our mothers
had;
said it was normal to feel; to need; to want.
made it difficult to breathe
and our teenage hearts swelled

with every verse;
broke for men we were yet to love.

Amy, did you ever think about us?

- **Ode to Amy Winehouse**

Lately, I am seeing red every day.
The anger in my blood. The knot in my throat.

Red is the colour of the sun at its most tired.
Weary with everything it has witnessed.
All of our ugly, unGodly ways.

Red is a heart beating in the chest of a refugee.
Fighting to live. Dying to survive.

Red is the colour of our children's limbs.
Worn and torn across strange new lands.

Red is the colour of fear,
the loss of life and home and peace.

Red is the colour of mercy.
The warmth of a stranger. The beauty in kindness.
The curve of a mouth that is shaped like home,
"you are welcome here."

Red is in everything lately.
The anger in my body.
The softness in my flesh.
The brown of my skin is tinted.

The refugee in me is haunted.

- Seeing red

Where do I go?
I am black, I am Muslim,

Where can I stand?
What part of Earth is safe for me to rest?
And where can I build a home for my babies,
away from guns and cops and angry white men -
who are always too insane to be held to account?

What corner of Earth is there for people like me?

- Target

What I know of war
is written on my mother's body.

I run my fingers over
the skin of her legs -

like secrets in Braille,
the wounds,
they speak to me.

- **What I know of war**

Breathing Just A Little

There is so much of her in me
this woman.
Stood proud.
Head dress forming an earthly hallo
about her voluptuous frame.

Her name is Nuura.
And she is light.
Forever radiant.

I have bathed in her sparkle,
basked in the twinkle of her love
and learnt the pains of a woman's womb-
broken whispers of almost babies
that made her lament
and retreat into herself
like a broken angel
or an angelic human
whispering in virtuous calm-
Bismillahi Rahmani Raheem.

They said that bleeding
would make me a woman
and loving a man
would make me bleed
a different kind of love.

She taught me that blood
could also break a woman
and that tears
made even angles human.

That humans-
sometimes came in the form of demons-
and demons- sometimes looked like friends.

That forgiveness
make's the broken -whole
and the secret to happiness
lay in gentle remembrances of
Laa Illaha illallaah.
the velvety chuckles
of man and wife.
And in the
soft caresses
between mother child.
Between her
and I.

There is no woman
like her.
Her name is Nuura.

And she is light.
forever radiant.

- Nuura

My mother smells like softness, dewy spring mornings; flowers blossoming into life and rainfall after a dry season.

I am reborn in her company, her presence alone strengthens my roots.

My mother's laughter rumbles like clouds on a journey; drifting partly on Earth but closer to heaven.

I think of forgiveness when she smiles. I think of heavens and angels and gardens beneath which rivers flow.

My mother is home. She is peace and stillness and balance. She is more than any of the words I have to offer; more than any metaphor. I will never love another being more. Want for a being more.

- **My first love**

That kindness is what I am known for,
that it is what they say about me when I am gone –
this is my idea of legacy.

That though I am not always funny,
nor wild or exciting,

I hope it will be said – that my manner was
inviting.

- **Revere me**

I don't know really
how it is possible,
but sometimes,
I feel as if there is too much of me.

Too much to me.
I am too much.

And some days-
I feel that I am not nearly enough.

- **Enigma**

Some days
it is the things
I hold beautiful,
necessary and vital that crush me;
that pull me into despair
and cut me down in half.

My culture, my faith, my family.

Some days, everything
is chains around
my ankles, my throat, my lungs.

>　I am static;
>　I am small,
>　I am wrong.

These days,
I cannot remember
what anything means.

- **Chains around my ankles**

Some mornings I wake
a fire in my bones
to set the world alight

- **Alight**

I feel deeply connected
to anyone who speaks English
as a second language.

And perhaps it may be
they know it better than their first-
but the simple fact that they - like me -
carry another world inside them,
another tongue-

makes the connections
far more soulful.

- **English as a second language**

I am more heart, than brain,
more mistakes than lessons learned -
more wounds, than wisdom gained.

I am tender and brown,
warm; summer glow -
melanin for a crown.

I am woman, soft.
I am black, light.
I am human, gentle.

There is no anger in me,
no violence in my mouth,
or fire in my eyes.

I am Muslim, peace.
I am artist, love.
I am nomad, heart.
I am alight with pride,

Burning with love
raging with all this tender inside.

- **Lit**

Some days it feels as if
my soul is trying to
break out of my body,

I am so little outside
and so much within,
I feel my insides burning.

My soul is boundless,
my *nafs* is a wild creature
that my body is struggling to time.

- **Soul break**

When I die-
do not forget that I was,
that I walked among you all,
that in some small corner of softened earth,
my footprints remain.

Do not forget me too quickly.
tell them about me,
those I never had the chance to meet,
even if just for a while,
tell them something kind,
something pleasant and true.

Say it soft and gentle
as if you are afraid
there is a chance I may hear you.

Do not forget me.
Keep me please,
Keep me alive a little longer.

- Do not forget me too quickly

If there are words
to be left in my memory,
or a speech to be made,
let it include the words
love and light.
Let it combine bravery
and fear in equal measure.
Let it start first with
a greeting of peace
and end in much the same,
let it be read by someone
who knew my prides as well as my shames.
And let them speak of God
as I believe Him to be,
using words like forgiveness and mercy,
kindness and hope.
And for the few I loved and loved wholly,
let there be mention of yesterdays,
single moments in history that shows
my love for them unmistakably.
If there are words to be to be left
in my memory,
let them be written English
but read in my mother tongue.

- In memory of

Sometimes I am struck
by an overwhelming
feeling of detachment.

I belong nowhere.
I belong to nothing.
I am nothing and no one,
nowhere.

- **Detachment**

The light

First,
the hardship
must break you -

Then,
it will make you.

- Resurrection

Let the quiet hold you my love;
let it mold to your being,
let the silence move you to a new understanding,
an enlightenment.

How will you find peace
if you are always running?
How will you find understanding
if you are always surrounded by noise?

Let the quiet hold you my love;
let it hold you a little longer.

- **The quiet**

I am only half the woman I know I am,
a quarter of the woman I desire to be.
We are growing still,
we are growing every day,

do not stifle your own petals,
do not deny yourself a blossoming.

- Blossom

I want you to know that everyone,
everywhere feels the same sometimes.
That loneliness is a human condition.

I want you to know that I understand.
And that sometimes,
connections don't mean to others
what they mean to you.

I want you to know that time is everything.
And that sometimes,
you'll have to wade through murky waters
to get to clearer sea's, it gets easier.

I want to tell you about happiness.
And loneliness.
That they co-exist in a cycle,
never appearing at the same time.
Always one, or the other.

I am going to tell you that they negate each other.
And that if you are to find peace
you must find balance.

I will tell you that solitude
can be both your best friend,
or worst enemy.
You must learn well when it affects you kindly
and when it hurts you.

You must know that exercise

will always be good to you.
Good for you.
If you are sad, run.
If you are happy run.

And I am going to tell you that being good,
is everything.
Even to those who hurt you.
Especially to them.

Because when all the feelings have settled
and time has passed,
you will look back and smile,
not at anything, nor anyone else,
but at yourself.
And how you made it through unscathed.

- **Loneliness is a human condition**

Write love letters though you may never send them. Always in your best handwriting, though they may never be seen.
Buy books though you may never read them, fill bookcases even if they only collect dust. alphabetize.

Buy instruments you might never learn how to play. Pluck the strings of a guitar as if you are learned. Press keys on your piano, pretend this is music.

Buy clothes you won't ever wear. In batches and bundles. Bunch them all in the bottom of your wardrobe until you forget you ever had them.

-

And if the letters make you cringe, ten years from now, burn them in your backyard. Burn every memory that ever made a dent in your smile.

Donate all the clothes and books to charity. Write small anecdotes on the inside of all the book covers. little pieces of wisdom for the next person who reads them.

And maybe when you are older and wiser, Maybe you will realize, that when you play any of your instruments, you've made a melody with all the mistakes along the years. And it still sounds every bit as beautiful.

Stop second guessing. Life is for the living. And you will never be more alive than you are right now.

- You will never be more alive

Sometimes, the winds will blow too hard,
and the nights will seem too dark-
some days the hands on the clock will drag
and you will notice all of the emptiness around
you.

This is when you must dance.
Even in all of this emptiness
you must dance.

- **Dance**

You are always looking elsewhere
for things already brewing inside you.
Like the love you seek in the arms of people who
only know how to touch your flesh without ever
reaching your heart;
and the validation you seek
from the 'almost friends'
you pour your feelings out to;
who only ever seem to leave you
feeling less than you are.

You are always looking for meaning
through interactions;
for reasons to believe in yourself,
through how others respond to you.
Like the relationships you tried to build
but failed to succeed at
and how much time you spent
wondering what you had done wrong.

You are always looking.
Always seeking.
Searching everywhere but within.

Isn't it time your real journey, should begin? Isn't it time, you start to look within?

- Finding love within

- Your face is beautiful. Your lips are full. Skin the colour of a rising sun- but your eyes are sad, brooding. Your smiles never reach them.

- You wear a smile that steals breaths from those who cross your path- but your eyes are empty. Your gaze searching. Always scanning through crowds; seeking. Always looking.

- Because you have never been able to forget the first time you were kissed. To forget the beating of your heart. The feel of cheek against cheek. Their smell. The touch of fingers against skin. The warmth in an embrace.

- Heartbreak taught you how to appear whole, complete. How to 'be' in moments without actually being there. How to smile as though your heart was never broken, How to search without being noticed.

- But time- time will teach you how to stop looking. And this will be the hardest lesson you will ever learn.

- **The hardest lesson**

Some days are for loving and living,
for making dreams and creating memories,
and some for working through the battles,
for digging and building a path to the top.

But in between there are days for resting
and nights for healing.

These are the most necessary of days,
do not forget yourself,
take time,
take a little time for you

- Take a little time for you

You are a body of water;
bigger than any ripple
another can make,
be still -
let the density
of your peace
be felt,
let the current
of your calm
flow free.

- Be still

Go and live in a country, far removed from your own. Don't stay in one place, for the whole of your days.

Learn another language - even if only the basics. Try. Choose a place that intrigues or terrifies you - a culture you know little about and move there. Pack for a year, even if you do not stay that long.

Speak to people and bond with them. Even if only for a moment in time - by facial expression or mime, connect.

Learn how to eat in this new land. What rituals are meant for which part of day. Learn how to greet; whether to shake hands, hug or kiss. Find what being alive means to them and how love is expressed.

Do not compare it to what you have known, do not belittle it because it is strange. Life will teach you that even strange, is relative. And you are equally as alien to those you find alien, as they are to you.

But even strange, is life. And even there, there is love and laughter.
What greater adventure can there be, than to find this out? What greater beauty, for a heart to see?
When humanity and kindness, transcends all barriers? Where learning a way, and teaching them yours, can bind?

When the shopkeeper demands that you must stay for tea, don't leave. Accept. Drink with him in his market stall. Have dinner with your neighbours and sit with them on the floor. Pay attention. Observe how they eat and eat like them too. With your hands, with sticks or even a spoon.

And if it becomes too much for your heart to bare. If the strange soil conquers your body and makes you ill - leave. Don't stay. Go home. Eat your mothers cooking. Sleep in the house you grew up in. See the doctor, who treated you as a child. Eat the food that grew your body this big, for a time.

And when you are better, and when you are well. And when you find yourself searching for the food of the places you've been. Or receiving strange looks from friends, for the new habits you've brought with you home. Pick up your map and try again.
No experience is a waste. However short or difficult. You may not see the change, while it is happening. But you will change, nevertheless.

But do not travel, intending to save the world. Do not presume, your way is the best way of all. Be open, be willing. Life has much to teach you still.

- **All this world awaiting**

There will always be people who love,
and there will always be people who are loved.
There is no shame in either,
and there is no weakness nor blame.
There is only hope;
that we can someday,
be both of these
at the same time.

- Lovers in love

Be soft
even in your aggressions;

watch the world
fall over itself
trying to figure you out.

- Tender mouth, fierce heart

Breathing Just A Little

It is insane, how much of ourselves we pour into others.
How deeply we love, hope and believe.
And how we gaze at our men,
all lazy eyed and opened hearts,
as if- their fingertips could caress open wounds
and soothe the heart of she who cannot see
how beautiful God has made her.

It is in vain
that we try to unearth the secrets of the universe,
that we learn the stars
as though God had left a map of our destinies we could trace,
we create charts.
Venus is of love-they say
and the meaning of life is whispered into the secret language of the winds.
but if we could only understand
if we could only understand, that this is all in vain.

That loving a man will not make you beautiful.
That he cannot love you, when you are incapable of loving yourself
and he can break you; leave you staring at the moon,
eyes reflecting a silent cry for all the times you've bled and all the times you've healed.
But you will heal and will live.
Just as the rain fertilizes a barren field,

you will blossom.

And you will come to know that there is no
fountain of youth,
the young, no more immortal than the old.
And the meaning of life is not concealed in the
hieroglyphics of ancient caves
nor is it muted by the murmurings of desert winds
but clear in the small mercies of every day.
A child whispering into the ear of his broken
mother
"everything is going to be okay".

That love is not written in the stars;
in the palm of a fortune teller,
or in the heat of a drunken moment.
But in the eyes of a man
who after thirty years of marriage,
still tells his wife that she is beautiful
and places kisses across the scars of where her
breast used to be.

You see
I have seen in the faces of strangers
a sign from God
that everything is going to be okay.

- A sign from God

When you are tired take off your clothes
everything zipped, belted or buttoned;
anything fastened or tied to your body.

When you are heavy, slip on something light and
comfortable, undo your hair,
let it fall loose in any way it wills.

When you are close to giving up, take off your
shoes and socks. Sit on the ground, on carpet or
the grass outside; be still.

When you are exhausted, body and soul, heart and
mind, it is okay to take a moment.

We are always going and going and chasing and
doing.

When you are tired, be still, you have earned the
right to have this moment.

- **Stillness as healing**

Don't tell anyone that you think you are ugly. Even if you do. And when the woman at the counter says you have beautiful skin, do not burn up a brighter shade. Believe her. Smile, say thank you.

Never reveal how much you hate the sound of your voice over the phone. Let the first boy who calls you like clockwork every night, listen to you fall asleep.

When he asks the next day, if you've ever noticed how your voice changes as sleep starts to take you, say yes. Believe him when he says, he could listen to you all day.

Don't say how much you hate your teeth when he tells you that you have a beautiful smile. Don't clench your lips together when he says your mouth makes him think of home, smile wider.

We all have parts of ourselves we'd like to change but we have parts of us that are beautiful too. Don't let the voices in your head, take you for a fool. None of this will stop love finding its way to you.

- **The voices in your head**

Breathing Just A Little

Softness

Everything about us is soft. Skin and water. Warm blood. Our entire existence is soft. Air and skin and muscle. Hands and feet.
We touch and it is soft; we love and it is warmth. We live; footsteps gentle against the land and even in our death; we are tender; wrapped in Earth and giving back to life.

Yet we are always pretending that we are strong. Rock hard. Immovable. Untouchable, as if there is something wrong with this softness, with this tender.

When really, it is all that is keeping us alive, stopping us from falling apart completely. You cannot mend a thing that is hard. You cannot fix it, when it is broken.

I am thankful for this softness. That keeps me breaking and healing. And healing once again.

- **We are soft**

Soft,
I am soft -
who is tender enough
to handle all of
my softness?

Gentle heart
and tender soul.

- **All of my softness**

I am only interested
in softness.

Softness
and sincerity.

- **Come as you are**

If you are ever wondering how you appear to me,
know that I think of you kindly. Lightly. Softly.
I think of you as brightly,
as I do of the sun.

I look for you as I look for the moon,
on these darkening nights;
and perhaps you do not find yourself worthy,
but this is how I see you always,
even on your weariest days.

This is how you look to me.

- **How you look to me**

I fall in love at first meaningful conversation
and first heartfelt interaction,
that subtle smile passed between us in a crowd
over some small thing we both found amusing.

I fall in love at first secret shared,
first fear revealed;
first painful memory during a quiet moment
in a busy place.

I fall in love as if I were a mermaid,
only into depth;
never near shore,
never shallow waters,
only ocean overflowing.

- **Drown**

Everything is burning,
every continent,
every nation,
every home,
everything is burning.

It feels like the world is on fire,
every inch of it raging.

I wonder what will be left of it,
when we are done?
And what will be left of us?

- **Up in flames**

Why should I carry
secrets around,
waiting for someone to tell,
when I can write them down
and leave them behind,
just as well?

- **Writing as letting go**

If it causes your blood to boil
you must speak up-
how many deaths have words
suffered in your mouth?

How many letters have you swallowed
and left to drown in your
cowardliness?

- **Speak**

Something about
a moment of
absolute silence
feels like redemption;
the world in pause,
life in stillness,
and breathing
and breathing
and being.

Something holy,
something grounding;
something like coming home to myself.

- **Grounded**

If you must love,
love with intensity-
love deep enough to feel
its ache in your chest.

Do not offer
your body to another
if your heart is elsewhere,
do not profess with your skin,
with your teeth, hands or lips,
do not pretend.

But if you will love,
do so entirely,
infinitely,
in truth.

- **Love in truth**

Sometimes in the quiet
I feel you;
as if you never left.

- **Gone**

Some days the tides
go against me
and I am battling against
a current too strong -
while others;
they flow with me,
I am at one with the ocean,
buoying along in perfect harmony.

It is not for me to question why.

Some days life will give
and some - it will withhold;
all there is to do,
is to react in equal measure.

- **Let the current guide you**

My femininity is strength,
my curves are sharp,
voice a piercing softness-
you cannot break me.

My spine knew of bending
before yours knew of strength-
there is no load I cannot carry.

- My woman is power

I love you in the quiet hours
and in the still of the night.

I love you in the morning haze
and in that first break of light.

I love you in pieces
and all throughout the day.

I love you, I love you,
what more is there to say?

- **In the quiet hours**

My heart is a delicate,
darling thing.

A warm,
wondrous place;

a soft,
timid space,

and I must do
whatever I can
to protect it.

- **Guarding my heart**

Of all the boys I will fall in love with
(though I don't believe there will be many)
I'll marry the one whose frame is jagged
but heart is soft.

Because what will I do with a man
who has never learnt that the strongest of men
are those who are softest with their women?

- **The strongest of men**

I think I've glossed us over in my mind;
painted us a tender and precious colour.

I think I've written us over and over again so often,
I remember us as glorious now,

isn't time a mercy?

- **With time we forget**

I am not afraid of the silence anymore,
it is in the quiet I have found a voice in me,
that I never knew existed.

- **In silence is truth**

End.

Printed in Poland
by Amazon Fulfillment
Poland Sp. z o.o., Wrocław